CONTENTS
- Page -

LINDA'S
- Foreword -

A simple change to your living room, garden border, or even your wardrobe is a quick and easy way to keep things fresh and moving forward. And if it's unique too, then so much the better! The projects in this book are designed to be eco-friendly, resourceful and of course easy on the budget. The items featured are taken from a selection of The Air Ambulance Service charity shops across the country and we have given them a new lease of life.

We want to change the way we see previously unloved pieces, and to show you how to sew, stick, splatter and salvage your way to unique and stylish upcycling. From freshening up tired t-shirts to revamping vases, this book is filled with ideas to inspire you to make something new from something old.

The best bit about upcycling is that anyone can do it: from fresh ideas for more seasoned crafters to quick fixes for glitter addicts, we've pooled our collective experiences and ideas into this creative guide to help you create personalised gifts, re-invent your wardrobe or home accessories, and keep the kids occupied on rainy days. We've also included adaptation options so that makes are appropriate for boys and girls at any age. If you're new to upcycling, we should warn you: it's addictive!

We hope you enjoy experimenting with these projects as much as our team has done, and that you're inspired to do the same. Pass it on, and the possibilities are endless!

*Love Linda Barker (Charity Supporter)
& The Air Ambulance Team
x*

TRADITIONAL
- Cake Stand -

Make your own cake stand to display your delicious baked treats. You can spray paint your stand any colour you like to give it a modern twist, or keep it vintage with pretty patterned plates and odd glasses.

You Will Need:

- Selection of plates and glasses *(we used three different sized plates and two glasses)*
- Glass glue
- Spray paint *(if desired)*
- Newspaper

Clean your chosen plates and glasses with warm, soapy water to remove any grease or dust. Dry thoroughly.

Plan out your chosen design to make sure your stand stacks up – larger plates and glasses at the bottom will help to make it really sturdy.

Spread out some newspaper to protect your work surface, then spray paint your glasses and plates in your chosen colour scheme. Refer to the manufacturer's instructions to make sure you get the best results. Allow to dry.

Once everything's dry, use glass glue to stick your plates and glasses together layer by layer. Allow the glue to dry completely before moving the stand. Finally, fill up your stand with a confectionery feast!

Other Ideas:

You could also use glass or ceramic paint for a more delicate look, and even fill your glasses with glitter, beads or buttons before you glue everything together for a truly showstopping stand!

TEACUP
- Bird Feeder -

Give your garden a touch of fairy tale magic with one of these teacup bird feeders! They make great Mother's Day presents and are perfect in any size patio or garden.

You Will Need:

- Old cup and saucer
- Super glue or impact adhesive
- Spray paint *(optional)*
- Newspaper
- Bird seed

Wash your chosen cup and saucer with warm, soapy water to remove any grease and dust. Dry thoroughly.

If you're painting your feeder, spread out some newspaper to protect your work surface, then spray paint your cup and saucer. Refer to the manufacturer's instructions to make sure you get the best results. Allow to dry.

Once dry, glue the cup onto the saucer. To make one like ours, position your cup with the handle facing upwards – this makes a perfect perch for the birds to admire their breakfast!

You could also decorate your feeder with artificial flowers or rhinestones to suit your garden's style – make sure these are well glued down to protect them from curious beaks!

Once the glue is completely dry, fill up your feeder with bird seed and make some feathered friends at the most stylish diner in town! They look great on a patio table too.

Other Ideas:

Go all Alice in Wonderland and try gluing your cup and saucer to old stair spindles and placing them amongst your flower beds, or hang your feeder from a sturdy tree branch using the handle of the cup. Use some metal chain (available cheaply from DIY shops) to ensure your feeder withstands a heavy blackbird!

This is a great make to get the kids involved, but ensure they are supervised at all times.

MEMENTO
- Box -

Hide your most precious secrets and treasures in this clever memento box, which breathes new life into an old book. These make lovely gifts for a friend and can be used to safely hold your most treasured keepsakes.

You Will Need:

- Unwanted hardback book
- Sharp craft knife
- Glue
- Envelope *(optional)*

Create a square template to use as a guide (the back of a photo frame works well). Make sure your template fits inside your pages with a margin of around 2cm/¾ inch on all sides.

Carefully use your craft knife to cut through the pages around your template. Keep going until you've nearly reached the back cover, or a shallower depth if you require.

When you have cut out the cavity, carefully tidy up any loose edges with your craft knife.

To secure the box shape, glue the last few pages to the back cover, and glue the bottom of a few of the cut pages to make your box really sturdy.

If you like, glue a pretty envelope on the inside front cover, to store letters or photographs. Make sure it fits inside the page cavity when the lid is closed.

Allow your box to dry completely before filling it with your keepsakes.

Other Ideas:

Why not personalise the cover of your box with photographs, drawings or sequins? You can also glue two ribbons to the inside edges of your covers (do this before gluing the pages together) so you can tie your box closed with a bow.

BEAUTIFUL
- Bunting -

Bunting used to be confined to village fêtes, but nowadays its popularity has soared! It's a great way to decorate a kitchen or child's bedroom, or is a fun way to style your party or garden.

You Will Need:

- Paper of your choice
- Scissors
- Ruler
- Pencil
- String or ribbon
- Glue or Sellotape

First, create a template to ensure that your flags are the same size. Simply use a ruler to draw your desired size triangle onto a piece of card, and cut out.

Use your stencil to draw as many flags as you need onto your chosen paper.

Carefully cut out your flags.

Cut a piece of string or ribbon to the length you need. Fold the top of each flag over your string or ribbon, and secure with glue or Sellotape.

Hang your bunting in place and stand back to admire your happy handiwork - voilà!

Other Ideas:

You could use wrapping paper to give a birthday party a present theme, or why not use old newspapers for a vintage look? Comic books will also look great in a little boy's bedroom, or decorate bunting with sequins and beads for a little girl.

DAINTY
- Table Runner -

Lace is hot property right now and perfect for adding fashionable finishing touches around the home. Check out your local charity shops for frugal finds, and remember that mismatched patterns are right on trend!

You Will Need:

- Lace doilies
- Fabric *(width and length to suit your chosen table)*
- Sewing needle and pins
- Matching threads
- Iron for pressing
- Buttons, ribbons, or trimmings of your choice

Measure your chosen table to decide the width and length of your runner – we used a runner about two thirds the table width and about 30cm / 12 inches longer than the table so the ends hang nicely over the table edge.

Sew a long piece of ribbon or decorative lace along the edges of the piece of fabric to cover up the runner's raw edges.

Arrange your doilies on top of the runner you've created until you are happy with your design, and pin in place. Then sew the middle of each doily to secure them to the runner.

Press with an iron to ensure all the doily edges lie flat. In case the doilies are synthetic lace, use a warm iron on top of a tea towel to avoid scorching the fabric (and a damp tea towel should help with any stubborn creases!)

Attach a button, sequin or stud to cover your stitches and add interest.

Proudly lay your table for high tea – the perfect opportunity to give your traditional cake stand pride of place!

Other Ideas:

If vintage fabric is discoloured by age or old stains, why not whiten or dye the lace to give it a new lease of life, or even beat old tea stains at their own game by soaking the doilies in cool tea. Dyeing the lace in co-ordinated soft pastels makes for a pretty vintage look, or draw doilies into the 21st century with clashing contemporary brights.

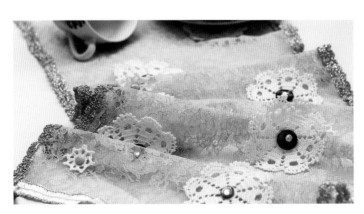

CREATIVE
- Headbands -

A headband is the perfect way to top off your look, and a unique headpiece is easy to create from all manner of everyday items. Simple headbands are great for children and teenagers, or go for glam with a unique fascinator.

You Will Need:

- Petal templates *(page 47)*
- Basic headband structure
- Fabric *(we've used an old red felt coat here)*
- Buttons or large beads
- Needle and thread
- Pins
- Glue & feathers *(optional)*

Trace the petal templates onto some paper and cut them out. Pin them to your chosen fabric and cut out five small, five medium and seven large petals.

For added interest, pleat the base of each petal by sewing a few medium length stitches and pulling the thread tight to gather or fold the fabric. Sew the five smaller petals together, making sure they're evenly spaced, and tie off your thread with a small knot; then do the same with the medium and large petals.

Draw about 60cm of thread through your needle until the ends are the same length to make a strong double thread, and tie a knot. Sew the three flower shapes on top of each other, largest at the bottom, smallest on the top. With the same piece of thread, sew a button or bead in the centre of the flower to cover your stitches. Still using the same thread, sew round and round your headband through the bottom of the flower to secure it firmly in place.

If you like, glue some feathers onto the underside of your flower to add some extra glamour!

Other Ideas:

As with all of our projects, this is just a starter for ten. From buttons, ties, fabric scraps and ribbons, to snippets from comics and magazines or miniature cards from your Christmas crackers, you can make flowers, bows and even fabric feathers to dress up a previously plain headband - your options are endless!

PERFECT
- Pots -

Lace trimmings can give old pots a fast facelift to make sure your patio's at its prettiest. White lace looks great against a coloured ceramic background, or go for a bright edging on plastic pots for a more pop art vibe.

You Will Need:

- Old plant pot
- Lace offcuts or edgings/trimmings
- Odd buttons
- Clear drying glue
- Spray paint or paint *(optional)*
- Old newspaper

Clean your chosen pot with warm soapy water to remove any grease or soil. Dry thoroughly.

If you're adding colour to your pot, spread out some newspaper to protect your work surface, then spray or paint the pot with your chosen shade. Refer to the manufacturer's instructions to make sure you get the best results. Allow to dry.

Paste a thin layer of glue onto the pot where you want to apply your lace. Press your lace onto the glued area and secure with a pin through the overlapped layers until dry. If you're using multiple strips of lace, make sure all the joined ends are at the back of the pot. Pull the lace tight around tapered pots to make sure the top edge is level, and you can overhang scalloped or shaped edging along a stepped pot lip to add interest.

Apply glue to the backs of your buttons and press into place.

Once the glue has dried, trim away any excess lace, pop your plant into your pot and admire your haberdashery handiwork!

Other Ideas:

Try using coloured ribbons and beads instead of lace for a more fun feel. Tired vases can also be revitalised with paper doilies, available in most supermarkets, and you can add an extra flourish with a ribbon bow, or an old brooch.

Once painted, these pots are great for kids to decorate with buttons and sequins using PVA glue.

BUTTON
- Canvas -

Channel Lichtenstein's dot pop art and make your own unique 3D button canvas! Eclectic buttons are always in vogue and readily available. Most charity shops and markets have a great range of inexpensive buttons, or you can harvest them from old clothing.

You Will Need:

- Buttons; various colours, sizes and styles *(the more the merrier!)*
- Clear drying glue *(hot glue gun or impact adhesive recommended)*
- Blank canvas *(available from most craft shops)*

Lightly sketch the outline of your chosen design onto your canvas in pencil. We've included a template of this stately stag design on page 47 - you could project the template onto your canvas with a lamp and trace the outline, or enlarge the template with a photocopier, attach it to the back of your canvas, and hold it against a sunny window so that the design shows through whilst you trace it onto your canvas front.

Once you're happy with your design, apply glue to the backs of your buttons and carefully stick them onto your canvas. We fixed buttons along the outline first, before filling in the middle areas. Depending on how dense an effect you're after, cover gaps by layering buttons on top of each other.

Allow the glue to dry completely before hanging your canvas on the wall, then stand back and reflect on your unique piece of art!

Other Ideas:

Use shades of someone's favourite colour to create their initials for a uniquely personalised present or a child's bedroom door. Remove an unwanted picture from its frame (keep it for paper craft projects) or cover the picture with some thick paper to create your own blank canvas: writing paper, wrapping paper or wallpaper are all picture perfect.

CUTE
- Coasters -

Give everyday coasters a vintage makeover with delicate lace stencils. Use two contrasting colours to mirror co-ordinated designs, or multicolour the lot with a consistent metallic lace pattern to tie the set together.

You Will Need:

- Old coasters
- Small paper doilies *(or trim large doilies to size)*
- Spray paint,
- Newspaper

Clean the coasters with warm, soapy water to remove any grease or dust. Dry thoroughly.

Confusingly, because you're using a doily to stencil your design, the first layer of paint (Colour 1) will form the pattern of the doily, whereas the second layer (Colour 2) will be your background colour.

Once you've chosen your colour scheme, spread out some newspaper to protect your work surface, and paint the whole coaster with Colour 1 (we chose gold). Refer to the manufacturer's instructions to ensure the best results. Allow to dry.

Now place your doily on the painted surface of the coaster and gently secure in place with Blu-tak or double-folded masking tape. Using your chosen background colour (Colour 2) – we used blue, pink and white – paint the coaster again over the top of Colour 1 and your doily stencil. Allow to dry.

Gently peel away the doily to reveal your design and use it to have a well-earned cuppa!

Other Ideas:

Juxtapose your vintage design with a grittier palette by using a black doily design on a concrete grey background. Or make table mats for Christmas lunch by cutting your own snowflake stencil from some scrap paper.

ALL TIED
- Up -

Charity shops often have a corner full of ties of all shapes, sizes and colours, at great prices. They're perfect for transforming something previously unloved into a one-off gift. These easily upcycled tie cases make great Father's Day presents.

You Will Need:

- Old tie
- Scissors
- Needle and thread, or sewing machine
- Tape measure
- Fastener: Velcro or press stud for a closing case, or ribbon for hanging case

To begin transforming your tie into something more useful, make sure that your chosen item (e.g. phone, scissors or paintbrushes) fits inside the wide end.

Measure the length of the item, and add on 7½cm/2½ inches (for seam allowance and to ensure a secure closing flap). This total measurement is the length of the tie you will need.

Now mark your totalled length from the widest end of the tie towards the skinny end. Cut your tie, and discard the excess skinny end – you'll now just be working with the remaining shorter, wider end.

Turn the tie inside out and hand or machine stitch straight across the opening you've just cut at the narrow end of your piece of tie, leaving 1½cm/½ inch seam allowance.

Turn the tie right side out again and press the stitched end with an iron to make sure it lies flat.

For a closing case, attach a fastener to the triangular end of the tie on the inside. Place the item inside the case and fold the triangular end over to form a snug closing flap. Mark where to attach the other fastener on the outside of the case, remove the item again, and sew on the corresponding fastener (perfect for keeping a phone scratch free!)

Other Ideas:

For a hanging case, make a loop of ribbon and sew onto the triangular point of the tie (never lose your sewing scissors again!) Or you could make a draught excluder or teddy by turning the case into a snake – sew a red ribbon tongue onto the triangular point of the tie and two button eyes on the outside, stuff the inside and sew up the open end. Sssssuper!

PICTURE FRAME
- Memo Pockets -

A place for everything and everything in its place! These cheerful memo pockets are so easy to make and can be used anywhere in the home. Use it for holding recipes or receipts inside kitchen cupboards or office cabinets, or make a post holder for the hall.

You Will Need:

- Fabric *(old scarves, jeans, table cloths or linen are all ideal)*
- Scissors
- Pencil
- Tape
- Staple gun or strong glue
- An old picture frame

Remove the frame's glass and backing board and take out the unwanted picture (you can keep it for other paper craft projects).

When you've decided how many pockets you'd like, lay out the fabric across the width of the backing board. Each layer will form a pocket, so make sure they're straight and the right depth for your purpose. Once you're happy, mark the layers' depths on the fabrics with a pencil and cut to size.

Starting with the biggest pocket (at the back/top), simply wrap the fabric around the side edges of the board and secure the edges and bottom in place with a staple gun or strong glue on the back of the board.

Repeat this process for each consecutive layer. If you're using glue, make sure it's completely dry before you turn the board over.

Place the board back into the frame and start filling it up!

Other Ideas:

Dress up your design with some buttons, old jewellery or ribbons, or make sure everything's easily located by adding labels onto each pocket. Who said filing can't be fun?!

CUSTOMISING YOUR
- Clothes -

Upcycling is cheaper than buying new and means that you'll be rocking something totally unique! Just cut off the legs of old jeans - ripped edges create a great boho look - then tie dye them, add embellishment, or sew on fabric patches to give your cast offs a new lease of life.

You Will Need:

You won't need all of the bits and bobs listed here – adapt your design dependent on the time and detail you want to put in.

- Jeans
- Fabric dye
- Stencil *(for painted designs)* or string *(for tie dyeing)*
- Fabric
- Fabric scissors
- Embellishments *(studs, keyrings, beads, buttons, sequins…)*
- Needle and thread
- Glue

Planning is essential to make sure you're happy with your designs before they're permanent – for more complicated upstyling, pin your additions in place and try the garment on to get an idea of what your finished item will look like.

We've sewn lace trimming and buttons around the pockets and hems. We also appliquéd some bunting-inspired polka dot fabric by using Bondaweb to secure the triangles onto the shorts, then machine stitching the fabric edges. For a hippy chick vibe, cut down some artificial flowers, glue in place and then sew the stems in place with strong or doubled thread to make sure they're super secure.

Other Ideas:

The possibilities really are endless! Rhinestones and beading look great on back pockets, or add some freehand doodles with fabric pens or paints. And you don't have to stick to denim – you could add beaded lacy epaulettes to a tight t-shirt or beaded collar tips onto a shy shirt to glam up your work wardrobe!

PRETTY PAPER
- Projects -

*You can use paper crafts to cover just about anything!
Use a map of somewhere special to create a beautiful
personalised gift. If you're lucky enough to find old
atlases in a charity shop, snap them up whilst you can!*

You Will Need:

- Old lamp
- Old map *(old road maps work well)*
- Scissors or craft knife
- PVA glue

Clean the lamp shade with a soft brush to remove any dust.

Lay out your map on a flat work surface, and roll your lamp shade across it to make sure the map area is large enough. Measure out how much of your map you'll need, and cut out the area leaving an extra 5cm/2 inches all the way round the edges.

Cut 5cm/2 inch deep tabs into the top and bottom edges of the paper, to ensure a smoothly curved edge when you fold the paper inside the lamp shade.

Paste a thin layer of PVA glue onto the back of the map (including the tab area) and carefully stick it onto the lamp shade. Make sure you smooth the paper out from the centre to avoid air pockets. Fold the tabs over the top and bottom of the lamp shade to create a smooth edge.

To reinvent your lamp even further, you could paint or spray paint the lamp base to match your décor.

Once the glue is dry, pop your lamp shade onto its base and bask in its cosy glow!

CLASSY
- Collars -

Stand head and shoulders above the rest! These collars are incredibly versatile and instantly dress up a plain t-shirt and jeans to seamlessly take your outfit from day to night. Experiment with different looks and radically update your wardrobe – no shopping bags required!

You Will Need:

- Collar template *(page 46)*
- Pins
- Fabric
- Scissors
- Decoration: buttons, beads, rhinestones
- Ribbon or old necklace chain with working clasp
- Needle and thread
- Clear drying glue

Photocopy the template onto paper and cut it out. Lay the paper around your neck to check it's the right size. If necessary, change the setting on the photocopier to reduce or enlarge as appropriate, or draw round the template onto another piece of paper with your modifications.

Lay your fabric out flat and pin your template to it. It's best to use non-fraying fabric (e.g. felt) for this project – if you think that your chosen fabric might fray, you could use Bondaweb to join two pieces together back-to-back to stabilise it.

Cut out the collar shape around the template.

Decorate your collar by sewing on buttons and beads, gluing rhinestones, or even incorporating old jewellery (this project is perfect for the more magpie minded!) It's best to plan out your chosen design before you make it permanent.

Once your decoration is finished, allow the glue to dry thoroughly. Take an old necklace and remove the clasp with about 10cm/4 inches of chain spare on each side (or you could use two pieces of ribbon).

Sew the end of the chain onto the tips at of the back of the collar using strong or doubled thread. Don your new collar with pride!

Other Ideas:

Little girls will love creating their own collars with PVA and sequins.

ON TREND
- T-shirts -

T-shirts have to be one of the most easily accessible items in charity shops, and we've all got faded favourites loitering in the back of our wardrobes waiting to be loved again. From appliqué designs to fabric paint stencils and prints, these ideas are an opportunity to wear your heart on your sleeve.

You Will Need:

- Old t-shirt
- Newspaper or scrap card *(an old cereal box is perfect for the job)*
- Fabric paint *(as many colours as you like!)*
- Piece of sponge
- Thick card *(to make your stamp or stencil)*
- Iron *(to fix your design into fabric – check the manufacturer's instructions on your fabric paint)*

Printing:

Lay out your t-shirt on a flat work surface and place a few layers of newspaper or some card in between the two layers to prevent your design from soaking through to the back.

Sketch your chosen design onto the thick card and cut it out to make your stamp.

Sponge fabric paint onto one side of the stamp so that it's evenly covered.

Press the painted side onto your t-shirt to ensure the paint is evenly distributed, then carefully remove to avoid smudging (although an even finish isn't essential – a patchy or smudged print can be part of 'the look' too!)

Stencilling

Sketch your chosen design (or print a design from your computer) onto some card and cut out the middle of the shape to make your stencil.

Place your stencil onto your t-shirt – pin larger or more complicated designs to make sure they stay put. You can make stripes by sticking thick masking tape straight onto the t-shirt.

Sponge fabric paint onto the t-shirt to create your unique design.

Repeat your prints or stencils to complete your design. When the paint is dry, use an iron to fix the colour into the fabric (refer to the manufacturer's instructions for best results).

Other Ideas:

Look to the media for inspiration and new trends! Statement t-shirts in handwritten fonts can be reinvented with fabric pens, or a fine brush and a steady hand! Or use everyday objects to make instant stamps – get creative with old cassettes, forgotten cutlery or worn out tools!

Let the kids get messy and create their own t-shirts, but ensure they are supervised at all times! It's better to let an adult iron the design too.

SHAPE UP
- Your Shoes -

Put your best foot forward and attach brooches, bows, buttons and even knick-knacks to make your shoes one (well, ok - two) of a kind! Let your imagination run wild in your local charity shop to make yours truly unique!

You Will Need:

- Some basic shoes *(less is more at this point!)*
- Glue gun *(or clear drying impact adhesive)*
- Decorative accessories: flowers, feathers, buttons, ribbons, brooches, trinkets – if you can stick it down, it's fair game!
- Fabric pen or paint, glitter glue, fabric embossing gel, or even nail varnish
- Laces *(optional)*

The method will change dependent on your chosen design but, broadly speaking, the following steps should guide you.

Make sure the shoe is clean and dry. Plan out your design roughly against the shoe – this is the most important bit, regardless of whether you're simply adding some buttons and bows, beading a more intricate design, or painting the soles. Keep any stencils or templates for future refurbishments.

To decorate the top of your shoes, work systematically so that you don't knock glued accessories out of line as you build up the decoration. We used a sheet of gems in a preformed pattern from a craft shop, but something as simple as an oversized bow in a contrasting colour and texture, or an old zip zigzagged across the top, can turn ordinary black court shoes into party heels fit for a glamourpuss!

Other Ideas:

Take inspiration from the shape of your chosen shoe and check out current trends to adapt to your own style. Toe capped ballet flats lend themselves to becoming cats and mice, whilst pointy toes make better foxes. Deck shoes' flat tops make great canvasses for fabric designs (get the Bondaweb out!) or transform sensible office flats into tie-back tasselled masterpieces!

Fabric pens and adhesive gems are great for kids to personalise their own canvas pumps.

INNOVATIVE JEWELLERY
- Holder -

There's a fine line between being fashionably late and becoming the Mad March Hare – it's always the last minute jewellery decision that pushes us closer to the latter! Chase away chain tangles with this handy jewellery holder.

You Will Need:

- Old cheese grater that's seen better days *(the blunter the better, for obvious reasons!)*
- Spray paint
- Newspaper

Spread out newspaper to protect your work surface.

With your chosen colour, lie the grater on its side and spray paint the inside surfaces. Refer to the manufacturer's instructions to ensure best results.

Stand the cheese grater upright and spray paint the outside making sure that all areas are evenly covered.

Allow to dry.

Get your rocks on and give your jewellery holder pride of place on your dressing table!

Other Ideas:

Bring on the bling by gluing on rhinestones and sequins after spray painting, or split the handle area into precious, costume and everyday jewellery space with ribbon dividers wrapped around the handle and tied with a bow. You don't have to stick to one colour either – use masking tape to section off stripes and spots using two spray paint colours.

SNUG
- Snoods -

The knitting renaissance is still in full swing, and is a fail-safe option if you want to create something totally unique. This pattern is simple, fast, and offers loads of opportunities to experiment, so it's the perfect cosy Christmas present for all your friends!

You Will Need:

- Knitting needles *(we used 20mm needles)*
- Chunky yarn
- Bodkin or blunt needle
- Buttons or beads for decoration

Cast on 16 stitches.

Work in garter stitch until the snood measures about 55 – 65cm/22 – 25 inches, depending on how snug a snood you're after.

Cast off.

Fold the knitted length around to form a tube, with one end overlapping the other by about 2½cm/1 inch. Using some more yarn on a bodkin, sew along the join to secure your snood.

Decorate the join with buttons or beads.

Slip on your snood, and stay snug and stylish whatever the weather!

Other Ideas:

Double up with normal weight wool in two different shades for a multicolour twist, knit a longer piece for a V-neck overlap, or work in moss stitch for an even chunkier finish.

WELL HEELED
- Shoe Bag -

Protect your newly festooned footwear with a smart shoe bag – perfect for keeping pairs together in your wardrobe or keeping your suitcase organised.

You Will Need:

- Old pillow case
- Needle and thread/sewing machine
- Bondaweb
- Fastening: Velcro, press studs, buttons
- Fabric scraps, ribbons, buttons, bows or rhinestones to decorate

Lie your pillow case out flat. The existing opening will be the top of your shoe bag. Lay your shoes on top of the pillow case to work out how tall your bag needs to be: measure the distance from the opening end and double it to leave enough fabric for the closing flap. Mark this point.

Cut straight across your pillow case at the marked point. Turn it inside out and sew across the cut end - this will form the seam of the bottom of your bag. Turn the bag the right way out again and press the seam flat with an iron.

Fold your bag in half and add your fastening to stop your shoes falling back out.

Now for the fun bit! Cut out a shoe shape from your fabric scraps and attach it onto the front of the bag – we used Bondaweb to attach the appliqué layers then sewed the edges of the shapes to make sure everything was secure before we sewed on our white bow.

Pop your shoes inside and get globetrotting in style!

Other Ideas:

Why not use the appliqué decoration to create personalised pictures of your shoes so you know what's inside at a glance! There are some shoe templates at the back of the book.

RAPID RENOVATIONS:
Panic presents, rainy day revamps & uncomplicated upcycling

SEW

Cover baking sheets with some spare fabric, hang with a ribbon and hey presto – instant magnetic memo board! You could even glue buttons onto magnets to complete the look.

Torn shirt? Cut off the cuff, sew together lengthways and use the button as the opening in a purse or sunglasses case!

Re-use old cardigans as cosy cushion covers. Just turn the garment inside out, sew a continuous seam in the shape of your cushion, trim away the rest, turn the right way through the buttoned front and dress your cushion in its new clothes! This also works well on cardis and jumpers accidentally felted in the washing machine... We're just saying...!

STICK

Chipped teacup? Glue the teacup onto the bottom of the saucer, turn it upside down and pop a tea light on top for an impromptu supper centrepiece.

Co-ordinate a regular memo board with your décor with some leftover wallpaper – glue buttons onto thumb tacks for the perfect finishing touch.

Bring the outdoors in by gluing hessian or garden twine around an old glass vase.

Stick an attractive piece of fabric into a redundant picture frame. Use a whiteboard marker on the outside of glass to make an unusual notice board.

SPLATTER

Paint old pots with chalkboard paint and use white paint to add your house number, or keep a track of your herb garden with chalked labels.

Style up plain plates with metallic Sharpies – draw on your design, bake on low in the oven for 30 minutes, and it's permanent! Personalised plates make great gifts for parents and grandparents, co-ordinate your crockery for a party, or give your girl a hen party platter she'll never forget!

Spray paint a selection of quirky ornaments from the charity shop in co-ordinating colours for a contemporary home showcase. In with the old, and make it anew!

Plain wicker baskets can be spray painted to embark on new lives as stylish storage boxes. Mix and match bright colours for a funky display, or keep it neutral for organised calm.

Swill a small amount of paint around the inside of a glass vase for an interesting display piece. Or use non-toxic glass paint to turn a random assortment of glasses into a set.

Revamp an old picture frame with a personalised glass print – just remove the old picture (add to your paper craft stash), and replace with plain paper to make your print pop, then paint your design straight onto the back of the glass, dry and put in the frame! Getting the family's handprints (and paw prints!) is a great project to start you off.

SALVAGE

Wrap chunky wool or string around old vases for a modern textured update in the perfect colour for your room and bouquet, or go for ribbon and buttons for a more feminine vintage look.

A pretty watch which has lost track of time makes a beautiful and unusual bracelet – just replace the insides with a photograph or picture (use black and white or sepia prints for a vintage look). You could even fill the gap with tiny beads.

Old salt and pepper pots make perfect children's glitter shakers.

Use an unusual tie as a neck scarf or belt and stand out from the crowd.

Old records can be really quirky placemats and great dinner party conversation starters - singing for your supper is optional! If your record collection is more vint-ARGH!-ge than hipster chic, conceal the evidence with some spray paint!

Old metal forks make eye-catching kitchen and tablewear accessories with a quick tweak. Bend the middle prongs back and the outer two forward and use as place or menu holders; or bend the end of the handle into a soft curve; attach to a flat pence top block, and drill onto the wall for kitchen hooks!

GLOSSARY OF
- Terms -

Appliqué

A decorative technique in which pieces of fabric are sewn onto a larger piece of backing fabric to form a design. Bondaweb can be used to fix the pattern in place securely before sewing along the edges of each piece in the design.

Bodkin

A long, thick needle with a ballpoint/rounded end and a large, elongated eye/hole, perfect for sewing up knitted projects with wool or thick yarn.

Bondaweb

A crafter's best friend! This double-sided, iron-on adhesive tape looks and feels a bit like a spider's web backed with greaseproof paper. It's great for making double-right-sided fabric seamlessly (which also adds body to the fabric and helps prevent fraying), as well as for securing appliqué designs in place before stitching their edges. Follow the manufacturer's instructions depending on the brand you use, but in essence, iron the Bondaweb (paper side up) onto the wrong side of your first piece of fabric; allow to cool; peel off the paper backing; place the second piece of fabric onto the Bondawebbed first layer, wrong sides together; iron the fabric sandwich; and allow to cool. It's as easy as that!

Cast On

You 'cast on' to start your piece of knitting. There are several different techniques of casting on – refer to one of the many knitting tutorial websites for a step-by-step guide that suits you.

Cast Off

'Casting off' is the method used to finish your piece of knitting securely. Again, online video tutorials are helpful learning resources.

Garter Stitch

Garter stitch is the simplest way to create knitted fabric, and is produced by knitting every stitch (as opposed to purling). There are many online tutorials and videos which show you how to knit stitch.

Moss Stitch

Knit and purl alternate stitches (all knitted stitches should be adjacent to a purl stitch; left, right, above and below) to create a textured pattern in your knitting. Refer to online knitting guides for a more comprehensive 'how to'.

Pleat

Permanent folds in fabric which are sewn in place to create shape. For the Creative Headbands on page 15, make several tiny folds in the base of your petal by sewing a row of stitches and pulling the thread tight to pucker the piece of fabric along the stitched line.

Seam Allowance

The area of material between the edge of the fabric, and the seam or line of stitching. It's important to leave a seam allowance so that if your fabric frays, the damage doesn't spread into the stitches and cause the item to fall apart!

CRAFT
- Templates -

*Templates for "Classy Collars" (see page 31)
Scaled to ½ the original size: photocopy the
templates at 200% to help construct beautiful
collar necklaces adorned with gems.*

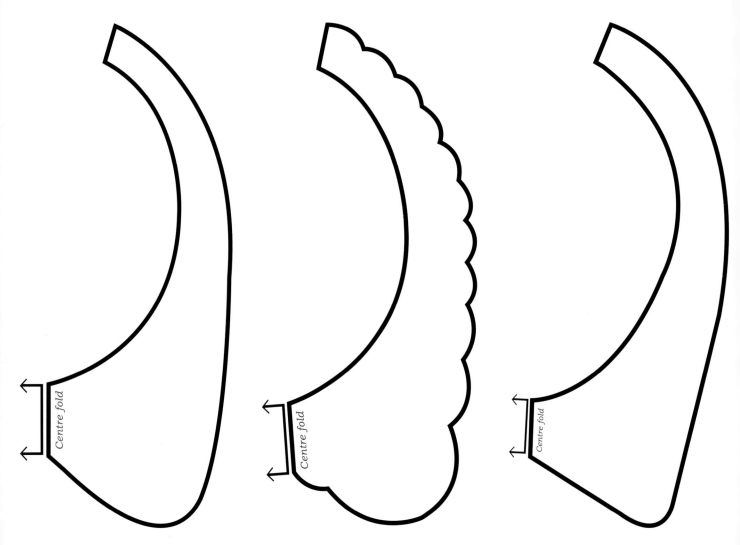

Centre fold

Centre fold

Centre fold

CRAFT
- Templates -

*A range of templates and shapes to embellish
any of the crafty makes within this book.*

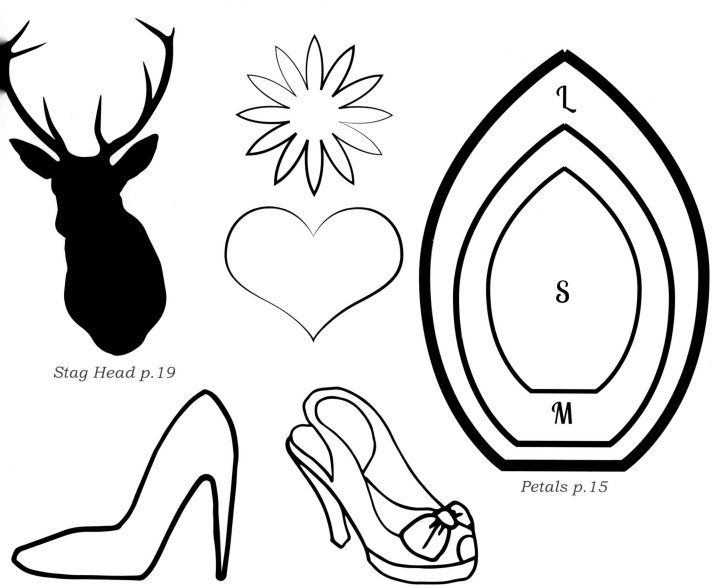

Stag Head p.19

Petals p.15

NOTES

- Pages -

NOTES

- Pages -

THANK YOUS
- & Dedications -

A special thank you to all those involved in bringing this craft book to life. We hope you enjoyed being a part of it as much as we did!

Author

Ellie Johnson

Designer

Alice Vaughan

Charity Supporter

Linda Barker

Photographers

Jake Vaughan
Justin Thompson

Printer

Technique Print Group

Air Ambulance Editorial Team

Kirsty Wayness
Lauren Bowman
Amy Valentine
Kerry Martin
Emma Vithlani
Krysten Swindells
Sue Pateman

Volunteers & Crafters

Britta Jarvis
Angela Wilson
Moira Jackman
Gaynor Haywood
Jasmine Mellor
Julie Wells
Gillian Chafia
Sue Kirk
Wayne Campion
Anthony Woods
Jane Vaughan
Irene Wayness
Oliver Ault